CONCORD

Vol. 5, 2013

Sandra Ellston
& Ruth F. Harrison, eds.

Acknowledgments

Carol Brockfield's poems first appeared in *Waiting for the Dark* (Oakleaf Press, 2012).

Gary Lark's poems are from *Without a Map* (Wellstone Press, 2013).

Bill Siverly's "Natural Area" was previously published in *Windfall: A Journal of Poetry of Place*, 11.2, spring 2013.

Margaret Chula's poems are from *Just This* (Mountains and Rivers Press, 2012).

Toni Hanner's "Two *Fin de Siécle* Indians" was published in *Moonmusic* (Wellstone Press, 2000).

Frances Payne Adler's "When Your Eyes" is from *Dare I Call You Cousin* and appeared in *Serving House Journal.* "Supreme" was published in *Global Poetry Anthology 2013* (Montreal, Quebec: Signal Editions/Vehicule Press. 2013. pp. 74-75).

Joan Dobbie's "Solstice Poem" appeared on a Christmas card by Chuck Eyers, 2003 & also in the anthology *Yoga & Poetry* (One Common Unity, 2012).

Sandra Ellston's selections are from *Poems Along the Way* (Turnstone Books of Oregon, 2012).

Ruth F. Harrison's "Fireflies live dangerous" appeared in *Tiger's Eye.*

Eleanor Berry's "In Defense of Analysis . . ." was published in *Seeding the Snow* 6.2 (Fall-Winter 2002) and "Inland from the Edge" appeared in *Ginkgo Tree Review* (The Ocean Issue, Winter 2012 – Spring 2013).

Judith H. Montgomery's "Saint Colonoscopy" was first published in *Ars Medica.*

Penelope Scambly Schott's selections are from *Lillie Was a Goddess, Lillie Was a Whore* (Mayapple Press, 2013).

CONTENTS

Keynote Address:
A Poet's Camino: How Form Follows Function
Ellen Waterston
May 3, 2013

Following in the footsteps of thousands of pilgrims, penitents, and seekers over centuries, last spring I walked the sacred ground of Spain's Camino de Santiago de Compostela in search of, in my case, answers to "What's next?" questions. This quest was prompted by stepping down after eleven years as founder/director of The Nature of Words, a literary arts nonprofit based in Bend, Oregon. A month spent walking alongside others with their separate sets of petitions, my worldly needs contained in a small backpack, seemed the right prescription for slate-cleaning.

It was never my intention to write about my experience, rather, as I walked, to determine which of the writing projects I'd been hungering to begin I'd first tackle on return. But the list of life questions I was *certain* I'd resolve while walking the Way was quickly supplanted by what the Camino had in mind, including, as it turns out, what I'd write next. When I got back to Oregon and was sorting through brochures and mementos of the trip, I stumbled on a map of the ten Camino routes that converge in Santiago. What jumped out at me, looking at that small map, was the stick- figure outline of a woman leaping.

In that moment Camino Woman was born in my imagination and she wouldn't let me go. She insisted on

1

being written. Here's an excerpt from my poem
introducing Camino Woman:

I am a leaping petroglyph, my she-shape traced
by the feet of centuries of praying pilgrims
filing across the rocky face of Galicia. My limbs
are sketched by the ten *caminos*. My stick figure
legs straddle Spain, the thin train of my dress
trails careless over the Pyrenees into France. One
of my olive-groved arms plumbs Portugal, the barnacled
other breakwaters the coast of *Mar de Cantabrico*.
Tied in eucalyptus, my long graying braids, *Primitivo*,
Plata, dangle across each of my mossy, cobblestone
breasts.

Fleshing out her fictional character, as the embodiment
of all holy women marginalized by patriarchal religions,
spawned other characters, other "voices", including a
fictionalized *pelegrina* "of a certain age"; a stylized and
profane Catholic church in Father Tomas; an omniscient
third-person voice; the role of the *hospitalero* as
wisdom keeper; and caricatures of others met along the
Way. The Camino is sometimes referred to as the *Via
Lactea*, a reference to the fact that the Milky Way is
always overhead when walking.   This observation
inspired a legend among early day pilgrims I describe in
the collection's title poem:

Via Lactea

It's said the Milky Way's but dust kicked up
by pilgrims' feet, the wheel-shaped star-city made

by *pelegrinos* walking. The shimmering arrow
of Sagittarius points to the middle of the misty
arch where sparkles and flares blend in giant curved
arms of gleam and Camino powder and ash.
The Sun teeters on the edge of this spiral fanfare,
fancying our distant world with ancient light
where luminous bands of the religious walk the trail
of ghosts in clusters, chains, ribbons. Each pilgrim
part of the same spiral story; each pilgrim's prayer,
a pinprick in the bag of obsidian night, writing
a new, bright galactic star-way, illuminating
the raven abyss.

But now the tongue of the galaxy grows thick
with time and distance. Less and less intelligible,
depleted Jovian giants bellow across light years.
They say: Wake from your arrogance, your tumbling
sleep, lest your El Nino oceans boil. Beware the outrush
of expanding notions of self, the rapacious black hole
of your greed. Even the present night is eclipsed by day.

Via Lactea, the title of the collection, will be published
by Atelier 6000 of Bend with a launch date of November
1, 2013—first as an art book followed by a commercial
run.

I tell you all this because, well, I'm excited *and* uncertain
(all the feelings associated with going public with
something one has created and that feels risky), but also
because in reflecting on the process of writing *Via
Lactea* what was intriguing was the dance between
form, both overarching and specific to individual poems,

and function. Hence, today's topic: A Poet's Camino: How Form Follows Function.

The first form that applies to this collection is that of the verse novel. *Via Lactea* is a narrative as told through the medium of poetry rather than prose, with characters...and a storyline that thread through it. A kind of a libretto. This is no edgy, post-modern genre as you know. The heroic epics (Gilgamesh, Iliad, Odyssey, Aeneid) set the stage starting in 10th century BC. Modern versions include Ann Carson's *The Beauty of the Husband*, *The Sugar Mile* by Glyn Maxwell, David Mason's *Ludlow.* And two of my favorites are Patricia Smith's *Blood Dazzler* and Frank X Walker's *Buffalo Dance, The Journey of York.*

What previous experience did I have with this form? None. The form found me. Just as the stick figure rendering of Camino Woman found me. Plunging in, as is my wont, I quickly encountered the pitfalls that poet Michael Symmons Roberts describes, the to-be-avoided presence of "essential but dull building blocks to get from A to B" or the crafting of a story long on music, short on narrative. How could I provide the necessary narrative information without the work going flat? Had I subjected every line of poetry to formal pattern and creative pressure so the writing didn't get soft in the middle? Working within this form turned out to be an exciting and humbling process.

No sooner did the Camino Woman show up as the muse, the verse novel present itself as the container, than the poems and their forms lined up along the trajectory of the narrative, like vertebrae along the spine of the story. In *Via Lactea* I wrote in free verse, came up with some new forms, and honored, reinterpreted and insulted traditional ones—all in pursuit of what I hope is a healthily dysfunctional result. (Maybe *that's* it. Form follows dysfunction.)

Former U.S. Poet Laureate Ted Kooser recalls a teacher who said "it is permissible to substitute a trochee or spondee or anapest or dactyl for an iamb, but only in the first or third foot, never in the second or fourth." This form business! Syllabic or accentual measure. Blank verse, marching in time with iambic pentameter. Nevertheless I was eager to try my luck. I learned to feel at home with the haibun, in one definition described as terse prose usually ending with a haiku. The haibun is also often associated with travel writings, is sometimes described as a "narrative epiphany" so it not only suited my style of poetry but also this walk, one that included journaling every day, that is after changing the bandages on my sore feet. The tanka, sometimes referred to as "short song," is best known in its 5/7/5/7/7 syllable count form. Its meter and shape on the page mimicked the robotic action, day after day, of walk, eat, sleep, walk some more, mimicked the isolation I sometimes felt on the trail. For Patricia Smith in *Blood Dazzler*, her powerful verse novel about Hurricane Katrina, the tanka fit the telling of drowned victims.

The breath just before
the last breath harbors the soul
encased in a verb.
I know the word by heart now.

Oh, I wish I could tell you.
Here is what drowning
feels like—God's hand smothering
your heart. And the thumps
grow slower, slower, until
He takes back your name. Lifts you.

Another form was the ghazal, built of couplets and repetitions. Its form mirrored for me the constant rain, day after day, while on the Camino. But free verse is my style, my righty *and* my goofy to steal from snowboarding lingo. Forms for me are hard, the way a New York Times crossword puzzle is hard. Robert Haas describes forms of poetry as numbers falling through numbers. For the form-phobic, they can be numbers disappearing into a black hole in space...unless of course you're David Hedges who humorously mourns the disappearance of poems written in traditional forms in his *A Guide to the Modern Sonnet*, appearing in the most current issue of *Verseweavers*:

Erase old-fashioned notions from your mind,
Frivolities like rhyme, unless it's slant,
And meter, because meter is a grind—
A kiss of death when going for a grant.
Now let you nimble fingers wade at will
In pools of unadulterated thought.
Express your inmost contradictions, spill
Your beans—but stick to business: Thou shalt not,
On penalty of death, write fourteen lines.
It's over, baby. Modern won the war.
Gone are the brick walls with the ivy vines.
New waves knock against the rocky shore.
Couplets, once considered groups of two,
May stretch from none at all to quite a few.

Despite the challenges, writing according to the strict dictates of a form forces word juxtapositions and rhythms that we might not otherwise be introduced to, and we can carry those conquered discoveries back to our caves. It's considered good for you to study the mechanics of form, know about rhyme and meter— just as steal cut oats are good for you, or liver, or interval work outs. But seriously, as we all know, the more tools in the tool box the better, so when a form comes calling, you can recognize and greet the unexpected guest.

The best of poets exemplify, and advocate, that the form of a poem must disappear, nothing should bring the reader back to the surface of the poem...most especially not a form that announces itself, overwhelms the content. "Every good sonnet is a good poem first, a good sonnet second," says Kooser. Poetry must lead and the form follow. Here's a fine example by Mark Doty titled

Golden Retrievals:

Fetch? Balls and sticks capture my attention
seconds at a time. Catch? I don't think so.
Bunny, tumbling leaf, a squirrel who's—oh
joy—actually scared. Sniff the wind, then

I'm off again: muck, pond, ditch, residue
of any thrillingly dead thing. And you?
Either you're sunk in the past, half our walk,
thinking of what you can never bring back,

or else you're off in some fog concerning
—tomorrow, is that what you call it? My work:

to unsnare time's warp (and woof!) retrieving,
my haze-headed friend, you. This shining bark,

a Zen master's bronzy gong, calls you here,
entirely, now: bow-wow, bow-wow, bow-wow.

But what is the genesis of form (including the very
important and often overlooked consideration of the
physical shape of the poem on the page, the feng shui of
it)? A brief look reveals, I believe, something of the core
function of poetry, of writing.

Coleman Barks says form is made of sound. The taste of
words, the taste of language delicious to the mouth. At
its core, maybe form is nothing more than a reflection of
the rhythmic signature within each of us. We, as poets,
are tapping time to our own rhythm and also to the
collective subconscious rhythm. "Nobody knows the
trouble I've seen, nobody knows but Jesus." Rivers and
drums, according to Kim Stafford. Short beats...and
long, uninterrupted ones. The study of other forms and
other poets introduces us to other drum beats, other
river sounds we can incorporate into our own writing.

Robert Haas, in discussing *A Little Book on Form,* talks
about bilateral symmetry: beauty and function. The
poet seeks what Haas calls "right ratio" in writing and in
life... of safety and freedom, of connected and not.
Recurrence and rhythm versus chaos. Being and
becoming. Haas asks: What is the question of the poem
and its answer to itself? And I ask: What is the question
our lives ask and our answer to ourselves? A poem, our
lives, can turn or stand still. A poem turns on its own
question. Verse *means* turn...of phrase, meaning, change

in rhythm and form. New forms emerge in the rhythmic patterns, the repeated going aways from some established sound shape or rhythm and then the returnings to the original pattern...like a child chasing and then retreating from waves on the beach. A poem, working within form then breaking out of it, is like the stages of child development from safe and dependent to individuation. That's the poem's job, or one of them, the poem's function.

It is at this point, it seems to me, form and function start to merge. The question we form with our lives is the function of our lives. Poems try and try for right relationship (form) to keep us and the reader of our poems awake and alive (function). We try and try to make our sense of ourselves and the world, meeting ourselves coming and going in the process of writing poetry. As Doty says: "If I don't give shape to my experience in language I don't feel real to myself." So, in the end, maybe the function of poetry is to give form to the poet and by association to the reader, to make Velveteen Rabbits of us all.

Here is a poem by Bob Hicok that I feel succeeds in that way:

Pilgrimage
                    My heart is cold,
it should wear a mitten. My heart
is whatever temperature a heart is
in a man who doesn't believe in heaven.

                    I found half
an old Barbie in a field

and bather her torso
in a coffee can of rain, put a deer skull
with antlers in a window
to watch with empty sockets
deer go by, these are souls
given the best care
I can manage, a [pigeon died
and I gave it to the river.
                              If lightening
loved me, it would be sewn
with tongues, it would open
my mind to the sky
within the sky.

        I put birds
in most poems and rivers, put rivers
in most birds and thinking, put the dead
in many sentences
blinking quietly, put missing
into bed with having, put wolves
in my mouth hunting whispers, put faith
in making, each poem a breath
nailed to nothing.

It was architect Louis Sullivan, the designer of tall steel
skyscrapers in Chicago in the 19th century, who coined
the phrase "form follows function", the form
determined by the purpose of and the audience for the
building. At the time it was a radical concept, eschewing
the old styles of architecture.

Every established form holds within it the exhilarating
invitation to push the limits so long as the integrity, the

structure, the true north of the work remains intact. In poetry (*and* in architecture if Louis Sullivan traced the origin of his idea) I guess I'd have to say I think form follows ignition, follows combustion, and that function plays a role once heat is being generated, and I'm talking **poetry heat**. Nothing like it. There's nothing in the world like it.

Camino Woman lit my fire, the actual path of the Camino de Santiago suggested a linked but staggered telling, and soon unique forms emerged. We, all of us, begin with a thought, an observation, with word kindling, consonant and assonant strips of paper, and suddenly the writing catches fire and our function, it seems to me, is to then *serve the poem*. We all know the feeling of looking at a completed poem on the page and wondering where in the world it came from, intimately familiar to us and a total stranger at once. Known each other forever and only just met. I feel that way about the gathering of poems in *Via Lactea* and have all of you to thank, as I prepared these comments, for a reason to reflect on their conception and birthing as well as broader considerations of form and function.

I close with: **Return to Sender**, something of a benediction and the final poem from *Via Lactea*:

Pretend you're an envelope
with a note inside written
in the form of a prayer. Pretend
the all of you, your em —
dash laugh, your run-on
mistakes, is the inscription
of a perfect petition written

by the Poet in His/Her elegant
metaphysical hand, then folded,
placed inside the envelope that is
you, and gently mailed into the world
when you were born.

Your prayer is written within
the within of you. The space
between each you-word
is where heaven abides. Asking
help from a distant deity
is a waste of time. Prayer
is a reporting, a telling. Every day,
if you can, turn more and more inside-
out so the you-prayer is exposed
to more and more light.

Thank you for the opportunity to be with all of you this
evening.

Ellen Waterston

Summer Lake in Spring: Ode to a Seasonal Lake
Now you sonnet, now you don't.

Look, now this fleeting lake's a shimmering silver platter.
What a kaleidoscope of changing patterns, flight and color.
Sweeps of blue, green, slate. Then brown and pitted by
rain's incessant yammer.
Plover, willet, swallow, gull dart and hover,

scavenge the seasonal mollusk, bug and brine—
that is until this Summer Lake's sudden, petulant winds
scatter the birds to shelter,
or her mischievous gusts conjure alkaline
dancers—veiled strumpets of chalk dust spinning helter-
skelter.

This temporal tarn has no choice but to indulge her every
mood,
adore her shallow reflection, succumb to each ephemeral
whim.
For she knows she has little time—neither for the
enduring mountains that brood
along her edges, harvesting wind and color from the thin

clouds that provision her evaporating palette; nor for me,
the petering poet who scans summer lake's drying alkali
flats and chimeric chorus lines
for too late meaning and too little rhyme.

Ellen Waterston

Horsehead Nebula
Now you sestina, now you don't.

Ah, the nebulae of persistent dreams.
And still I hope? Hope, like rainbows, is absence
perceived.
The sun doesn't set. Instead, the world recedes.
I'm but a gaseous figment in the eternity of self.
Whatever I believe, I see. A sea horse? Or a horse's
head between Orion's buckle and belt?

I pretend 3-D when there is none, pretend earthbound
and securely belted
in. Instead , only one gravity-less dimension, a dreamy
Dali-esque world of puff and dragon, hoarse
from silent, fireless roaring. This non-existent pony-
perceived
remains deadpan, expressionless in space, a mockery of
a self-
centered universe, its tongue thick with distance. But
against all vaporous odds it reseeds

hope in me because I will it so, races to deliver the news
to the next galaxy, the last receding
into the future past. The invisible rider exhorts speed
with his belt.
I feel it across my body, wear his constellations,
flagellations on the haunches of my self.
My inner thighs are bruised from his gripping passion,
the dream-
shaped scar above my eyebrow from galloping into his

arms full-speed, bare and horse-
back. The ringing in my heart now? Reverberations of
him, that knave, that whoreson.
That ringing sound— the frail receipt
I carry long after we have turned back from what I
perceived
was him dancing the rascal dance, celebrating, shouting,
belting
his favorite refrain: Love is all! How I wanted it to be so.
Some veils should not be lifted, some dreams
not chased. Some notions stolen from inner space of an
imagined other and self

better left there, shelved.
Safer to opt for hopeless. Be a headless horse
man, sleep a dream-
less sleep. Let dreams gag, recede,
strangle them with the belt
of reason because, over time, I have again and again
perceived,

again and again have perceived
these notions of love and self
are but vapors. That glistening star-studded belt
of Orion not yet born, dead already; that horse
head nebula receding
faster than the speed of light into the ether of idiot
dreams.

Dreams finally perceived for what they are reveal a
foolish
self that recedes from a self more foolish still, riding in
space
a belted bucking horse in free fall. The best things in life
used to be.

Carol Brockfield

1942

They took me to a war movie.
Black and white,
the best colors for terror.

There, bombs were falling,
crashing through roofs, walls,
everywhere with a flouring of debris.

There must have been a plot—
heroism, hope in despair
victory of spirit.
And more characters—
a mother, a father . . .

But what I remember is the little boy in pajamas
who ran from his black room
when the sirens screamed
and the building trembled
hugging a stuffed toy like the one I slept with.

Lamby wet his knickers, he confessed
Did *your* lamby wet *her* knickers?
asked my parents, laughing,
without even seeing my face.

Carol Brockfield

In a Polish Cemetery

Tourist and driver, we search
for that one name
across the field of sleeping markers,
weathered letters like runes
now fading with the day.

A bell sounds to toll last light.
Quiet as bones we hear it out—
the hollow cadence
the echoing intonations
the spaces between—
until the air is still
and lowing cows take up the dirge
insistent and mournful.

Like speechless stones we stand.
Dark drops across the valley.

Carol Brockfield

War Torn

When they marched again into Poland
I lay in my crib
looking at the dogs on my wall.
Family gathered in the other room
to listen to the news.
Mother, grandmother, aunt, uncle
pointed to places on a worn map. Touched them,
tongued their names and
the names of those left there.

Cigarette after cigarette fueled
bitterness, accusations in their private tongue:
Germany! Our friend! Betrayal!
Smoke and war talk overran the kitchen,
surmounted the walls
invaded the place where I lay with my pictures—

where Dachshund, Spitz and Schnauzer
pinned there to occupy me stood proud
in their purebred row.
It was the mutt
homeless, frightened
who held my eyes.

Carol Brockfield

Talk About the Old Days

Mention Poland
and I will turn to you, agree.

Yes, the constant cawing of those wretched crows
the broken hotel room TVs,
the Communist ladies at the bank,
post office, railroad station.
So rude.
So officious.
So lazy.

I'll break in
whenever you take a breath:
That ubiquitous Warsaw grey,
the weeds that push through city sidewalks,
the starving Russians selling used brushes—
shoe brushes
toilet brushes
toothbrushes.
And you'll say, *Even the babies never smiled.*

We never speak of Jasna Gora,
the wild virgin mountains,
the free-running Dunajec
or amber—that glowing resin
that captures the ageless—
the ancient and the beautiful.

Gary Lark

Hard Diplomacy

He was my father's age,
still tall and sinuous
with glinting eyes
and haunted dreams.
Bataan lived in his blood
like a virus: the retreat,
half rations, the capitulation,
miles of thirst, dysentery,
the everyday random death.
He had carried a friend
the last twenty miles
only to see him beheaded.

He slept with a Ruger .44
under his pillow.
It had a special sling
in his truck.
His wife had talked
him through thousands
of nightmares.
In 1976, with cancer in his gut,
the best surgeon in our
small town, one David Tanaka,
was to operate.

He surrendered to anesthetic
while the .44 rested in his wife's purse.
Through a colostomy

and another surgery
there came a hard diplomacy.
The son of a Japanese family from Fresno
treated him with respect, with deference
for the driving story that lived
in this man.

The patient lived another twelve years,
now and then stopping for coffee
with the enemy.

Gary Lark

Road Work

Tammy's divorces line up in her mind
like a trail of wrecked cars.
They'd been fixers mostly,
trying to fix herself
by working on someone
worse off than her.
The semipro football player
when she was eighteen
is still out there
trying to make it big in real estate.
She used to see him
when her mother was still alive,
his suit jacket thinner
and shinier each time.
And Jake. Jesus. Fat Jake.
He was all Santa Claus
when they got together
but after the wedding bells
he had to keep track of her
every minute of the damn day.
Two years after she left
he fell over dead,
a deep-fried time bomb.
And Willy, her slow-eyed mechanic,
with cracked, crusty hands
just nodded off.
He'd feed and sleep
like a barnyard sheep.
Still may not know she's gone.
Tammy looks at the trailer next door,
her hands in the warm dishwater—
maybe she'll start dancing again.

Bill Siverly

January

As we cross the Willamette, fog walls off the city in white.
In North Portland, frost forms an inch deep on sidewalks,
parked cars, and trees. Julia in the back seat says,
"Opi, it looks like snow!" "Frozen fog," I say.

Julia is always hoping for snow to close school,
to bring relief from grey damp days of January.
Years ago snow would last for days or weeks,
but we live in a different world now.

Allo-parent that I am, I ask the allo-kid
what global warming means to her.
"When gasses make earth hotter and there's no more snow,"
she recites, without hesitation.
As long as she has many parents, she can live without snow.

One more degree of warming, already underway,
melts ice-sheets and raises oceans. Four degrees,
when Julia turns my age, will transform her world:
warm rain, mountains bare of ice and snow.

Allo-parent that I am, I don't tell Julia what will come.
At home I show her how to raise her own salad and potatoes,
before our cool climate migrates north with all it grows.
Moonlight forms on rooftops like the ghost of frost and
snow.

Bill Siverly

Natural Area

Back in the '60's Mrs. Foley's horses would slip the gate
and go clattering on the asphalt up Lancaster Road.
Children and homebodies would chase after them,
and lead them by their manes back to their clearing.

Tryon Creek's ravine pastured livestock as long
as anyone could remember. Old-timers who grew up
above its wild rose and blackberry thickets recalled
the clank of cowbells passing below at dusk, again at
dawn.

When Mrs. Foley died in '96, Portland bought her place
and designated it a "natural area," meaning the city let it
be.
My dog Wolf and I always pause upon the decrepit
footbridge
to study the headwaters of the creek, polluted but clear,
broadleaf maples a simulacrum of the forest that might
have been.

Way before anyone can remember, the same creek
flowed
through old growth cedar and Douglas fir, now long
gone
to early logging operations. Fish and bear departed
with them,
leaving stumps to coyotes, deer, and a raucous flock of
crows.

Portland left Mrs. Foley's house slowly rotting in the
rain.
Wolf and I listen for the voiceless sound of being,
a sound like nettles sprouting out of mudbanks in the
spring.
Mrs. Foley's clearing is where Earth comes home again.

C. Steven Blue

Arms Of The Present

I am by no means the judge
don't wish to be the jury
I just want to lie here in your arms

I am no longer angry
or full of fury
I am simply bedazzled by your charms

Just lying here
in the arms of the present
no longer in the past

Trying to learn
from each new moment
trying to make it last

I am not longing
to touch tomorrow
I smell the scents of today

I know that tomorrow
will be taken care of
for someone is leading the way

Just lying here
in the arms of the present
no longer in the past

Trying to learn
from each new moment
trying to make it last

C. Steven Blue

Wildweed

My stuff is rough
It's bare bones
I hate to answer
Telephones
I want to look you
In the eyes
When we speak

But it ain't no use
In this fast paced world
To ride a horse
Or court a girl
If you take your time
To get there
She's just moved on

And what becomes
Of the alley cat
On the night
Of the hard driving rain
When the lightning speaks loud
And everyone crowds
In the shelter
Of warm window panes
I live my life
In a pot-bellied stove
I'm an oak tree
With ages to tell
I'm the earthquake commander

A green salamander
A salesman
With nothing to sell

But did you see me
On the night of the new
When everything changed
In an instant
The air was so clean
And the grass was so green
That a new age
Did not seem so distant

In the quiet
An angel calls
Awakened...
By the engine stalls
Of the inner city
Pondering its sleep

The dream is a draftsman
A hill-dwelling craftsman
A step in a puddle
On the road to forever
And life is a boat
In a great castle moat
We all circle
Yet must row together

Now is then
And yesterday's tomorrow
But how can we live it
Like we mean it

When we're running so fast
That the race cannot last
And the space in between
Lies unseen

Or is that to lay
In a meadow and ponder
The meaning of
The wild blue yonder
The stars at night
Or a daffodil
The momentum is great
As it rolls down the hill
Of imagination
Gone to seed

I'm a wildweed !

Why do I feel
So safe in the rain
And long to sit
Behind waterfalls
I gaze at blue crystal
I tell tattered tales
And listen...
When eternity calls

Maybe this just goes
On and on
Or maybe the hunger
Can't fathom the dawn
It's the spark in the dark
Behind your eyes
When you sleep

Just the moment...
And then it is gone

And you weep !

Sheltering skies
Pour forth from your eyes
And germinate the seed
Of my fast growing need

I'm a wildweed !

David Filer

Shining Back

I see you there, shading your eyes, the evening
Serengeti sun
shimmering
In the day's remaining heat. Something is out there,
soaring,
or gathering around
A carcass, or knee-deep in a watering hole. It doesn't
matter.
It's all too
Far off and lost in diminishing layers, the plain blending
into
the sunset
Beyond the farthest point that you can see. There, in
that farther
landscape, is what you came for:
The other, the out-of-place, the grain that is the least
and most
of what can be seen.
And it is there, shining back with its own light into your
eyes.
I see you turning,
Climbing into the truck, the dusty road, the clear, cold
earth-
circling air, touching down
In our green Northwest, what you've   seen still
there, as you come
toward me and your eyes meet
mine.

David Filer

Appraisals

Be careful, she said;
I am fragile, like
glass.

No. Fine crystal,
I said, and with my
wet finger, rubbed her
til her edges sang.

David Filer

Weather Patterns

Even on a day in which there is no rain,
The water is coming up,
and falling down.
River and breath, tear in the lover's eye.

Try January, wait for a dry day
And walk wherever your thoughts take you.
See if you don't come back soaked.

David Filer

Wild Roses

Rosa gymnocarpa

Here it is, mid-March,
and against our black
northwest skies, beneath

white gulls' graceful sweeps,
the wild roses bud
between sharp grey thorns.

Yes, now the scaups and
buffleheads will feel
the urge to head north,

and, still to the south,
goldfinches make their
summer plans. Winter

cannot hold against
such sure burgeonings;
and though cold rain streaks

through bare cottonwood
trees--wild roses bloom,
as we knew they would.

David Filer

Evening

Every old thing is with me...
Reginald Gibbons, "The Voice of Someone Else"

Every old thing is with me, when I let
The evening in, with all its histories.
Venus just now an hour from her set,
Bright above hills and fog. Wind skims the trees,
Hissing as if static, and then signals
Coming from somewhere, crossing the space
Imagination frames, pulses sweet and full,
Like memories I know I should not waste.
Where are you now, what have you learned,
That you're here in this unfamiliar place?
I'm looking west, to a sky growing dark
And cold, all but the planet's lamp-like trace.
Somehow your faded voice has touched me here.
How distant love can be and still be near.

Sue Fagalde Lick

Department of Motor Vehicles, 1945

"These days you wait in line to get in line.
It took four damn hours to get my license,
and I had called first for an appointment.
It didn't used to be that way. When I
got out of the service, my license
had expired. But I was driving a bus,
taking all the cherry pickers to work.
I drove fire trucks overseas, crash trucks.
Hell, I could drive just about anything.
So I left the bus in the parking lot,
went in and talked to the man at the desk.
'How'd you get here?' he asked. 'I drove my bus.'
He looked out the window and there it was,
perfectly positioned between the lines.
'Well, son, I know truckers who can't do that.
Take the test. I bet you'll pass.' And I did.
I traded my wrinkled Army license
for a shiny new civilian one, and
climbed back into the silver Peerless bus,
glad to be picking up cherry pickers,
happy to be picking up anything
that wasn't broken, bloody, burnt or dead."

Neal Lemery

Kilchis Point Walk

The trail leads me away
into the quiet of long ago
towards the bay
into the forest, where the wren calls
and two hawks soar above.

Through a marsh, dry now,
waiting for fall rains, a shower of
falling leaves covering my tracks.
Soon salmon will be in the creek
struggling upstream for renewal.

 Spruce grow bigger, taller,
shading the ferns, crowding out the
salmonberry, until only dark mossy rooms
remain, much like long ago.

They lived here once, those who came before,
in long cedar homes, tending fires,
living their lives with salmon, elk, and eagle.
Tides still come in and go out, and rivers rise and fall,
and salmon come back every year, on Spirit's time.

I hear them now, proud Killamooks, Chief Kilchis, too,
their canoes slipping up the bay on incoming tide,
all pulling together, all singing their song,
the laughter of children greeting them on the beach,
home again, and dinner almost ready.

Silent now, except for Wren, Chickadee, and obnoxious
Crow,
and the breeze off the bay, fresh with the change of tide.
The warm smell of summer almost gone, last night's
rain bringing promise of the winter, the storms,
the dark nights, and the fires of the long house.

I think I smell the smoke, see the peak of the longhouse
roof,
and hear the women sing as they pick the last of the
berries
before tomorrow's storm, and next week,
the return of the salmon,
as it always was, and will ever be.

Vincent Moretto
an inmate at the Oregon Youth Authority prison in
Tillamook

The Friends We Make

I cannot put a price
On this friendship we've made
And I wouldn't give it up
There's nothing I'd trade.

You treat me as equal
As one of the crowd
Even though I'm obnoxious
And vocally loud.

You accept me as I am
And you listen to me
Even though I'm young
and show immaturity.

In the past when people
Would drive me insane
You were the one there
Who helped me maintain.

I just want you to know
I cherish what you do
And the world could use
More people like you.

 -- dedicated to friend Rick Cobb

Dan Raphael

Alexandria

if rupert murdoch believes something
if wall street wants to roll 1-sided dice
congress and/or parliament will sing harmony :

if science and history are on sale what about all other
non-experiential truths:
just cause its on tv, on the web, in a newspaper--how
did it get there?

do everything you can to save the libraries full of books.
you cant change books, you have to burn them

you cant change books, you have to burn them

Dan Raphael

We have Nothing to Fear but August Itself

clouds are all about wholesale, squeezing the supply til
bonfires of umbrellas
promise a seller's market, rewarding rain with
exuberant nudity,
cats rolling on the driveway as if the rain is mama's big
tongue
cleaning where even the most contortionist cant.

the morning clouds that always vanish by noons full sun
are like the sign behind the bar promising free beer
tomorrow.
weathermen base their predictions not on the future
but what hasn't happened in a while,
when people start looking up rain on wikipedia, dial 1-
800-get-rain,
miles of clothesline flapping with what seldom sees the
sky.

sprinklers cant emulate what falling thousands of feet
does to water, all the stories it accumulates,
bird itineraries, poufs of rare metals, enough liberated
skin to plug a drain.
from the last storm i made contact lenses so i can see
rain that's not here
walking faster than the sun-drenched & thirsty, thinking
my sweat
fell from the bright blue clouds camouflaged by artificial
sunlight.

every week it takes a little longer to get this glass half-
full.

the mayor went to the ocean to offer incentives but no
one would see him,
they were on a team-building retreat planning the
surprises, the inch and a half during rush-hour,
the 30 degree drop making the leaves think they missed
their train before they could find their luggage. as if the
sun inside my refrigerator ever goes out, ever stops
serenading its contents
to sweat a little more, lose their water weight & be
ready to dissolve in the first mouth that finds them.

i'm getting long distance charges each time i open the
tap.
i wont believe anything the clouds say.
so much rain gathered in so few places, nothing
trickling down,
but such poignant jingles & finger-pointing--rain for
votes, rain for veterans,
families lining up before dawn at the water bank
knowing the naiveté of our empty gallon jugs

Dan Raphael

Pull Apart

the city around me pulls apart, as if a three dimensional
jigsaw, exposed fingers unclasped
and only i roll through un-pulled   poled   pawed
my
wallet
confirms my
location
parallel threads occasionally pulled into conflict,
probability strings--

sometimes the rain must leak to benefit the house; each
escape is a trade-off,
each change in currency effects fashion, ways to make
any face seem 2-dimensional,
5% taken from my pay check for future cosmetic
surgery
when windows are eyes and chimneys noses, architects
striving to make houses
that cant be mistaken for anything else—wombs,
nests,   bus shelters,
minivans without wheels,
the box from a giants refrigerator,
abandoned beach
houses turned into prisons,

if our roof is flat something
should be growing there,
hidden courtyards no human has stepped in for decades

　　　　　　lush with rodents and birds
all the scenery pulls away and where am i,　my car
　　　pulled away,　perhaps my body
　　　　　　but not me

　　　　　　　　　　II

evaluating something by how it pulls apart, a different
　　　　　　way to get where we started
cabbage　bread dough　remagnetizing a car so parts
　　　　　　repel each other,
giving a family member a new personality then seeing
　　　　　　what happens around him.

i ride my horse into a town that surprised me. i can tell
　　　　　　by how folks stare
i don't look like myself, not known from experience but
　　　tales, from transplanted memories,
　　　pictures by an unknown hand
　　　　　　　　　　the smell stays until
　　　　　　the sun wanes.
i open all the windows to the moons photonic wind--we
　　　did not come here to hesitate.
each resistance another rung to full muscular
　　　　　　blossoming.

　　　　　　buddha could lift an elephant with his
　　　　　　serenity.

　　　　　　　　　　III

think of a body as bondage;　think of a city as an
　　　　　　incubator.

43

as if being 10 or 100 feet higher when you sleep will
free your dreams from street level,
no one can float in when youre seven stories up
i want a
city where i can
jump between
rooftops.
the biggest dangers cant climb stairs--alligators on
elevators.
multi story condos wrapped in white plastic make me
nervous about whats really inside:

i inhaled so much that year i didnt breathe again til april
i felt radiant as a map of a place no ones been.--
antarctica de-iced
after the world's magnetic reversal—too many people
south of the equator,
too much waste hidden in the open.
i want to buy blue sky
install a sunlight dispenser inside my ribcage.

as i run the sidewalk collapses beneath me I fall into a
unnel
but see myself on the surface
city is a collage,   a
mutual agreement,
a moment frozen in mime,   since i
never get close enough to go in,
car tuned to destination,
where im authorized to reappear
city of implants   city of bottled water   city
where no ones outside for long
ask for directions to another city.   hold
your breath til the speedometer says 35.
that red lights not for you.

Dan Raphael

Still Hearing It

i don't want that 100 passenger salmon making an
emergency splashdown
in the accumulated mountain skin & silt of my life
stream
red doesn't mean go until you cant
thinking how a moraine cracked stream is the oceans
natural opposite
that an upstream death is better than one where
everything accumulates—
so much space with no ones name on it
til that morning
when everythings not what you want
tvs changing stations with every heartbeat
each hours shadow burns a new alphabet

haunted by a past that wasn't mine, dreaming in Polish,
unable to control myself in restaurants with live fish
tanks
or distinguish falling acorns from bullets
back when most nights the sky would tell the same
story
and I knew the sun was in my blood revolving through
my earth dark heart.
i knew that if i got three days from home I might never
get back
take the wrong mountain pass and im no longer
articulate or legible,
my cloak no longer matches the trees, streams wont let
me step in them
    i eat without shitting but feel light as a songbird

Scott Rosin

Evolve, Now!

If they can put a man on the moon -no
if they can put mouse genes in strawberries
why do I have to wear this wetsuit

I'm not saying
I don't have gratitude
for the damn thing

it's allowed me some joy
I'd surely have missed
in these chilly climes

but even the best are straitjackets
energy-sucking second skins
as slowing as extra gravity

pulling surfers down
like full-body galoshes
who wants to ride in mollasses

so- how 'bout a pill instead
a little gene-altering lozenge to help us out
when we want some cold water fun

just a temporary fix is all I ask
a synthetic hormone doobah
for a couple hours of warming relief

something to keep the cold out
by swelling the subcutaneous cells
beneath our hides

into a sort of happy human blubber
not too thick of course
just a few mil to wall out winter

wouldn't have to be permanent
no need here to buy bigger clothes
just engineered for a two-hour session

followed by a swift reduction
fifteen minutes and back to shore-size
in the walk from ocean to auto

'course the magazines wouldn't like it much
current skinny surf-heroes
looking a bit frumpy in the photos

less lean and mean more seal-like smoothe-boys
and a tough sell to the women
no desire to appear as so much bikini-clad sausage

the wetsuit manufacturers would howl
like buggy-whip salesmen
when the horseless carriages rolled out

but we all love progress and while we're at it
how 'bout a little something
to improve lung capacity and lower heart-rate

an improved mammalian diving reflex pill
for those long dark tumbles in the impact zone

an end to lung-bursting uncertainty below
the ad-men could have some fun here
Sub-Cu and Polar-Bare and Geneta-Suit and
Marine-Genes and Cell-Overalls and Surfer Skin

and ExpandaLung and Oxy-Gene and SubSurfer
and BreatheLong and Surf-Gills and DiveDeep
and Give-Em-Air

but dude why stop there
I could use wider feet and longer too
something more like flippers

and how 'bout some finger-webbing
and longer fingers while we're at it
to get some speed out on the briny

heck how 'bout some dope to fuse our legs
into great 'mongous temporary tails
to zip us out and charge the big ones

wouldn't even need a board at all
at Jaws or Mav's or Cortes Bank
forget tow-in jet-skis or rescue craft

we'd be out in hurricane surf
riding hundred-foot faces
banking down the biggest barrels

hot-dogging the heaviest hooks
blowing the minds of startled roughnecks
out on storm-battered Texas towers

or screaming past storm-tossed super tankers
while riding rolling water-mountains
as they march across the heaving horizon

and racing across massive pitching peaks
past wallowing cruise ships with throngs of
head-lolling tourists puking over the railings

listen man we'd be out in every condition
wilding among the wildest waves
upon all the seven seas

and after such sessions
when we were like normal
as normal as surfers ever are on land anyways

with legs and stuff
all happy and tired and wasted
as only the hard-core can be

we'd go somewhere warm
and sit down with a brewski
and talk and talk and talk about it

Christopher M. Wicks

Villanelle 19

If less than need, still more than mere desire:
The impulse sending me again to you.
One may decide to be consumed by fire,

And it does seem my straits are near so dire
That I have little choice of what to do
Besides obey this need, or this desire.

It is an option to accept the pyre:
Once immolated, nothing's left to rue
For those who have been all-consumed by fire.

The boundless pain once over, and the ire
Appeased, of gods and powers, false or true –
Why then, was it a need, or just desire

That made me seek to flee the hissing choir
Of all the flaming tongues, and wish to sue
To angels to deliver me from fire?

Only when you soothe, I do not tire.
Your healing balm like Springtime's moistening dew
Draws me with force like need – or mere desire?
It stills my fears, and calms my inner fire.

Cynthia Jacobi

Neruda Comes Out in National Poetry Month, April 2013

His disinterment has added irony to April -
another casualty unearthed from Chile's
dirty war. Let us hope the resurrection
was respectful honoring his place
in eloquence. Desiccated remains
were sliced and sampled, tissue
smeared on glass slides.
Suspected cause of death :
poison by injection. Political
cause of death : fear of words
from Poet of the People.

So you have come out, dear Pablo,
unveiling your body of knowledge
and leftward leanings. To counter
the sacrilege of your exhumation
I propose sky-burial
on Mt. Ojos de Salados, your bones
shrouded in a woven wrap of poetry
and wild wreaths of clouds.

Cynthia Jacobi

Photo at Silver Lake 1947

Though they had already lived a lifetime
here they smile, young and fresh.

He – returned by sheer luck from Anzio.
She – nursing in Veteran's Memorial wards.
My tall uncle in slouch hat, one eye shaded,
his legs so long his crotch was at her waist.
My aunt – gazing up – wavy hair clipped
back on one side like Lauren Bacall
in shorts and saddle oxfords, left knee bent,
looking saucy, one foot half out of her shoe.

Hefting brown bottles of cold Schlitz
they lean into each other. They adore.

I know now what they could not.
I know of their life well lived with candles
at dusk – of a marriage ended
with his death preceded by strokes
and marathon rehabs. If effort were all
he could have raced with Kenyans.
I know about her – miscarriage
after miscarriage – of how she delivered
one little bloody inchling
into the toilet and how she saved it
for the priest. I know for both the joy
at last of a healthy son. I know
of her final years: blind and near deaf,
She talked to him every day
but couldn't say his name.

Karen Keltz

Miasma

November's wind blows at the gate
Mid-morning Math, she clumps in late.
Her mother's heels with pointy toes.
Snot glissading from her nose.

No socks to bundle blue-tinged skin.
Mud-splattered knees, scab-covered shins.
Ripped fingernails engulfed in crud,
One scuffed-up elbow oozing blood.

Long, tangled, ropy flaxen hair
Falls over eyes that vacuous stare.
Blind but not blind. Dense or dumb?
She rubs her crusty eye with thumb.

Her azure satin dress, a wreck,
Hangs slack and filthy from her neck.
Mid-calf it falls, ripped at the waist.
Stained pilgrim collar trimmed in lace.

Our teacher sits her by the grate,
No punishment for being late.
She smiles at us. Our hearts are stone.
We do our math, leave her alone.

At recess time she wants to play.
We laugh at her and run away.
Confused, she chases us. Stops. Stands,
But we ignore her outstretched hands.

Ghosts like her leave soon, we know.
We hoard our love, dispense more woe.
She is not there, nor her despair.
Our hearts on hold, she turns to air.

Karen Keltz

Futility

His back to the front door, he chooses not to look out any window
but straight ahead at the TV where he watches cable news all day,
oblivious of what's happening right outside. She sighs more than once
and turns up her own TV two levels louder ten feet away,
in the living room, the Seattle Mariners and her "Ichi"
or the NASCAR races and her Kasey Kahne. All day,
WEATHER and NEWS and NASCAR and BASEBALL,
dueling ear bombs. Sometimes old Chuck Norris re-runs
are on both TV's. Neither hears the phone or the doorbell.
"Oh, I didn't hear you drive up," she says to company.
"You must have been quiet," but everyone letting themselves in
slams the back door and the brass bell tied around the knob jingles.
He keeps staring at his TV even when he mutes it for visitors.
He can't hear much anyway.

She won't buy herself hearing aids
because he refuses to wear his.
He won't wear them because then he doesn't have to
listen to her.

He doesn't like the chair she bought
so she won't buy the one he does like.

If he looks outside, he will have to think about
how he can't walk or drive or even wheel anymore.
How he can only sit in this stiff-bottomed wheelchair
minus its footrests and not even feel his nose run half
the time.
How no one talks to him anymore so he folds up
further and further into a "C" until his nose touches his
knee
and his lungs refuse to work so the oxygen kicks in
and he's someplace else, oyster shucking or worming a
hook
or plowing down by the slough.
How the garden plot sits there barren, topped with sun-
sucked-dry weeds
and desiccated cling peaches his grandson picked up off
the lawn
and pitched into a pile because not even the deer would
eat them.
How if she dies first, he'll lie there, rot and starve
before anyone notices.

How what he wants waits in the shop
but he can't get there,
to the rifle and the bullets.

She tells everyone she hates when he gasps for air
moving from chair to pot or chair to bed.
"He doesn't have to breathe like that," she says.
She goes outside to smoke and feed the cats,
smoke and take out the trash,
smoke and get some fresh air.

Every task ends in arsenic and tar.
Her hopes and desires curl up into ash and soot,
swirl round the patio roof and ride the wind.

She thinks about her promise made
when promises came easy and the promise now,
when keeping him at home means wiping the shit off his
ass
and sweeping his god-damned crumbs off the
floor. She'd rather
lie in bed mornings and read a book instead of laying
down
his medications before him one by one, like the choo-
choo train
she'd like to hop right on out of here.

She wants the same thing he does
all day long or when he yells her name at night,
but she doesn't know where he hid the bullets.

Amy MacLennan

Muggy

The air outside strokes
my hair. Hothouse
climate, locomotive
vapor, summer kitchen
kettle, overheated
engine haze, rainforest
mist, winter shower
steam, translucent fog,
sky close, clouds low,
gauze chandelier.

Edwin Good

Song of Songs 3.1–5

translated
[spoken by the woman]

In bed at night I sought my life's love,
      sought but didn't find him.

So I got up to go around the city,
      its streets and squares,

seeking my love;
      I sought but didn't find him.

The watchmen found me,
      who roam around the city.

"My love, you've seen him?"

I had scartcely passed them
      when I found my love.

I held him and wouldn't let go until
      I brought him to my mother's house,

  the room where she conceived me.

I put you on oath, Jerusalem's daughters,
      by the gazelles or the does of the wild,

don't rouse or waken
      love, until it wishes.

Margaret Chula

Six Short Poems from "Just This"

*

Vicks VapoRub
the smell of Mother in winter
her hands rubbing
my small chest back and forth
deeper into my heart

*

you sign your letters
'affectionately'
   I write 'loving you'
   picking a scab in my cleavage
   I watch it bleed

*

my parents and in-laws
moving toward senility
suddenly
there's no one
I need to impress

*

cleaning out
Mother's lingerie drawer
the tears in her stockings
sewn up so tightly—
all my unanswered questions

*

months after he's gone
the bar of Ivory soap
    in his bathroom
        still holding
the shape of his hands

*

displayed in the window
            of a consignment shop
        my old evening gown
    on a flaxen-haired manikin
the size I once was

Henry Hughes

Least Sandpiper

Sparrow small, streaked and quick,
down from the tundra in the graying slick. Least,
maybe,
but a whole flock is a big idea, turning tight to whim and
wind,
the delicious green rind of the bay.
Pick and probe, eat and eat.
Peep-voiced and unafraid, they alight beside us mucky
clammers,
shucked by the cute company. Pick and probe, eat and
eat,
then up-flock—
white bellies, black backs, white, black, white—
in and out
of our lives.

Toni Hanner

After Dreams of the Dead All Night, My Father

I wake late, bones aching and stiff.
A busy night of dead sisters

and living sibyls, a mother
somewhere, stirring the pot.

My ignorant calendar tells me
to send my brother a birthday card.

He'd be 76 on Wednesday, catching up
with our sister, now both are ash. I bought

tiny cork-stoppered bottles, thinking to collect
everyone, line them up on the mantle,

now I'm not so sure, I have my father, maybe
he's all I need, my blood,

my horse, shambling through family
in a flail, a smolder. The parentheses around

my father and me raising the hair
on the back of my neck, I conjure him,

he strides hobble-gaited through all the watchkeepers,
they can't see him and if they did, he'd seem a fool.

Inside the pale gold glass, ash sticks
together, wanting to hold some form,

Toni Hanner

Guayabera

I have almost nothing of my father, one white shirt,
guayabera style, ruffled and stiff, he would wear *for
good*—
holidays or out-of-town relatives. He'd take a bath

in two inches of hot water, slick his hair with Brylcreem
and shave the stubble from his face. A Stetson hat and
he was
good to go, jeans ironed crisp and so blue they shone,

boots the color of old blood. He was sharp.
You could cut yourself on him. And didn't he just know
it,
coming in late to make an *entrance*, everyone turning

from their games and conversation to his *Halloooo.*
He was always somehow unexpected,
as if we thought he couldn't possibly still be with us,

that disheveled twig we'd seen last time we visited his
house,
dust so thick you could pick it up in your hand,
roll it in a ball like lint from the dryer,

not that ancient stick in his ripped pants splotched with
paint,
his flannel shirt worn so thin you could see right
through it

to the waffle-weave long johns that warmed his cold
bones.

Aluminum walkers stashed in corners, canes and home-
made
implements to help him reach or stand or climb,
TV sets on in every room, the lullaby murmur of
baseball

carrying him all the way through October.
He smelled. No other way to say it, the house was
filled with the pungent odor of polecat,

a wild tang that made your eyes water as soon
as you opened the front door. So when he cleaned up
for company, it was as if he was new, younger,

an altogether different man, smelling of cologne and
hair tonic,
his white shirt flying from his skinny shoulders like a
flag.
We could pretend, then, that he would live forever.

Toni Hanner

Two *Fin de Siécle* Indians Lost in the Diaspora

(for my Dad)

Our tribe may be
down to two
we could
name ourselves —
the *Many Cats Clan*
or the *Eats Spaghetti for Supper People*—
we can make
ourselves up
Pop
just you
and me—
I'll be your Indian
if you'll be mine.

Jana Zvibleman

Back Seat

Once you've filled almost exactly inside the lines of the
princess's ball gown blue blue and her hair yellow in your
new coloring book, and you've peeked over at your sister's
and hers is prettier and none of *her* crayons broke, and
you've pretended all the trees next to the highway are getting
cut off by the line at the top of your window, and your daddy
has sung *Oh wee –eel of for–chun, keep spinning around*, again
and around again, and you've sucked and chewed the very
last raisin in your little red box, and your sister has shoved
your foot back to *your* side and she's made a face at you and
your mother has said *only to you* Keep your hands to
yourself, and you've picked the scab off your knee with
nobody seeing,
once your Daddy has sung *La Dee Da Dee Da Dee Da* some
more and you've asked while slanting your eyes up with your
thumbs if you're almost at Howard Johnson's *yet* and can you
get two scoops of pistachio *why not?* And after only 91 *Bottles
of Beer on the Wall* your sister has made your mother make
you change songs and you get only up to *The Ants Go
Marching Eleven by Eleven* when they tell you to stop that too
so you whisper loudly *100 Bottles of Ants on the Wall* til your
til your mother says Blow your nose and reaches back your
Daddy's folded-up white handkerchief and you've stuck it out
your window and held onto one corner tight and watched it
open *flap flutter wave and flutter flap a wing a bird a pretty
dancing dress a waterfall ocean you as a lady . . .*
then your Daddy says put that thing inside, I already told you
once, people might think you're waving a white flag for help.

Kelly Eastlund

Six and Twenty Blackbirds

Flecks of ink in bare trees, blackbirds
haunt the schoolyard. Swings hang red,
plastic-still over untroubled snow, silence.
We pretend we have answers, but blame,
like birds' posturing racket, moves on, leaves
tail feathers to fall, land, make no difference.

Who are we to think we know the difference
between grief and greed? When blackbirds
fall from trees; like leaves
twirling, we cycle through green, gold, red.
In autumn's dear dying, winter feels the blame,
retreats into silence.

Once I found eight feathered bodies in silence,
drowned in a tub of rainwater; no difference
to anyone but me, who took the blame.
Yet still I wonder about those blackbirds,
why eight small hearts, wild and red
as love, floated cold with sodden leaves.

Another headline, another shooter leaves
us shattered. Sorrow floods nights' silence,
Christmas lights strung green and red.
We sing a song for difference,
for six and twenty blackbirds
incapable of blame.

Gray is the color of guns and blame,
green the sound of trees unfurling leaves,
absorbing shadows of the blackbirds.
Other birdsong will grace the silence;
reveal a world that forgives difference,
its heart cracked open, a blood-red

elegy for all we've lost. No red
apple on the desk; no more time for blame.
We seek to grasp the difference
between truth and fear. As leaves
feed off light, spin sanity from silence.
Above the school now, blackbirds

fly into memory like pressed red leaves.
Beyond blame, act from the healing of silence;
know that makes a difference to the blackbirds.

Betsy Fogelman Tighe

The St. Petersberg, FL Cigar Factory Employs a Reader

My first season I heard:
Uncle Tom's Cabin, The Adventures of Tom Sawyer,
and became an American, retelling at the dining table
to mi madre y padre, my dark-haired hermano.

In the hot belly of the factory, bent over my box
of tobacco leaves, stacked and supple, fattening
beneath my strong fingers, plump as the palms
that swayed by the sea where we would swim on
Sunday,

El Lector, gifted with a drum-rung voice,
rang in the news, perched on the tall stool
in his white suit and panama hat, filling us with tales,
bearing us the new world as we worked to make it rich.

Presentando: *Song of Myself* and "The Belle Dame sans
Merci,"
Shakespeare's sonnets, the English a weapon with
which
I would win a wife, a woman proud to have a man
who could roll off a word or more to secure her
surrender,

roses and candy inferior tricks for wooing, less potent
than the words' elixir, which seeded the garden where
I would live with her. *The Scarlet Letter* and *Walden:*

el lector shook all our hands before he started, and
when the sun was no longer high in the windows, as we
packed away
the layers of leaves and pushed our chairs under, we
thanked him, singing a song or two that had carried us
across the roiling waters,
lullabies for him to present to his daughters.

Frances Payne Adler

Supreme

"A petition was filed to the Israeli Supreme Court to let Palestinians
harvest their grapes, and the High Court told the Army that they
must let them harvest... People have rights
to this land and there's no law that takes these rights away."

- Avital Sharon, an Israeli lawyer with Rabbis for Human Rights

Atta wants to go harvest his grapes
and he can't go because what used
to be his vineyard, the settlement took
as their *shabam,* their security zone,
and he can't go because he doesn't
have a permit and he doesn't have
a permit because they won't give him
one and this is the problem, so I
called the Army and they said he can't
get a permit because he has to prove
this is his land and he has to get an
expert to show that this is his land
and I said that he did that, he came
to your office and showed you the map,
and he said I don't have it, and I said,
could you look again because he even
remembers the date he was there and
Palestinians don't usually remember
the date and he called me back and
said, yes, I have his date, but I don't
have his map. But a map costs a lot
of money, I said, could I send it to you
on the computer and he said, no, I don't

like that and here's what we could do,
I could come to his land and you and I
and him, we could walk and he could
show me. So we agree on a date and
Atta and I are there and this guy doesn't
show for the meeting, and here we are,
this has been going on for three years.
Last year, they let him come in to harvest
his grapes, just for a day or two, and you
should've heard his voice on the phone,
calling from his vineyards, picking his grapes,
the joy. And now he wants to go in again, and
they're saying ever letting him in was a mistake.

Frances Payne Adler

When Your Eyes

*5 am, Qalandiya checkpoint,
between Ramallah and Jerusalem.*

You can barely see, at first, in the dawn light, working
men jump from buses, race to get in line, the banter
between them. You can't see the signs like in a dream
when your eyes won't open. What you *can* see are men
bundled against the cold night air, men who jostle,
shove, climb the steel bars, try to break the queue, men
who pray, who face east, kneel, press their heads to cold
concrete, all who wait for the gate to open. And then you
hear it, a few words slipping from lips -- parched wells,
the *wadi,* permits denied for cisterns, permits denied
to build a bakery, and *when you do, the bulldozer.*
What you hear is the gasp rising, the not-so-slow
stifle. What you see are soldiers, teenagers, some
in their twenties, machine guns slung like satchels
over their shoulders, their boots clacking the concrete,
and no one moving to open the gates. What you hear
are students in the 'Humanitarian Line,' *It's for nothing
you're filming us. They come, they film, nothing changes.*
What you hear is the silence of a woman wearing
a black *hijab,* who carries a sac of books in her arms.
What you see is a man who clutches his side and tells
you, *I wait here, away from the crush. I got my ribs
broken last week in the line.* What you smell are figs
in the fingers of a child, her father beside her, *I'm
taking her to hospital in Jerusalem,* he says to you

74

in Hebrew. And when the interpreter translates,
Her name is Pella, you hear her whisper in his ear,
Baba, I need to use the bathroom, and there is none.
What you hear is a businessman with three daughters,
taking them to school in East Jerusalem. *What,* he
says, waving his arm at the steel bars, the soldiers,
the guns, *are my daughters learning from this?*

Joan Dobbie

The Dog Died on a Daily Basis

One day it died
& then the next day it died again

On the days that it didn't die
Those were the days left for mourning

But there wasn't much time left for mourning
There was always a new death

After a while the baby started dying as well
Dog death and baby death

Then came the leaving of lovers
They came just to leave

They left you and then the next day
They left you again

It was a kind of a daily rape
It was a kind of a daily hell

I don't know what you did to deserve it
But you must have done something exquisite

The baby was thrown in the garbage can
The dog was buried with great fanfare
The lover was welcomed & welcomed again

It was always the same lover
It was always the same dog
It was always the same baby

You can abort it again & again & again
But the baby comes back
It is always the same baby

The soul, so they say, never dies

Joan Dobbie

Solstice Poem

Black & white wear each others' clothes
& the darkest moment is that moment

when the dark
lets go

The thing to do, I guess, is love the darkness
Knowing darkness also disappears

& trust the light, though it comes & goes
& makes no promises

Quinton Hallett

Dear heart

alien
pot-bellied stove
you bagpipe
root ball
pig bladder
you Africa
& South America
you gang of four

let me take
your pulse
press my ear
to you
I could listen
forever to your
subterranean
beat.

Nancy Hager

Two Haiku

A robin lands, rests
on my hand.
Our softness fits.

An eagle flies beside me,
eyeball to eyeball.
Quiet snow.

Sandra Ellston

休退

East of Town
(after Wei Yingwa)

I've been cramped
within my cubicle all year—
what relief to venture beyond the town,
toward the pure light of the rising sun.
Wind through the willows
whooshes a sound of peace;
the tall dark mountain
dwarfs my stressful angst.
As I settle near a thicket
to muse beside the stream,
it is fit to find my self.
Mist wafts a fragrance of healing
as the turtledove echoes her song.
Cheerful in seclusion, alone beats my heart.
Time and again I've obeyed
the call of work—
scheming affairs
that hurry me along.
Oh, to retire here!
To build a sturdy hut,
and like my old friend Tao
live true to my own nature,
genuine, ordinary, apt.

Sandra Ellston

回答

A Reply to the Young Mayor
(after Wang Wei)

Now, in old age, I seek the quiet life,
to free my mind of the ten thousand things,
contained within myself, just here and now.
In leisure I'll wander back into the woods—
winds through the pine will tug at my sash belt.
As moonlight floods the mountain
I shall pluck upon my lute.
What logic guides this life of poverty?
Ah, do you hear the fisher as he sings?—
so deep and rich!

Sandra Ellston

岩

Among the Cliffs
(after Han Yu)

Up the narrow mountain path
through stony crags, bats flit
in twilight as I reach the temple,
ascending the great hall. Good
to rest upon the steps after the rain
by huge banana fronds and lush geraniums.

The monk tells me of murals, portraits
of our prophet. His torch
illuminates the ancient face
holy and sacred underneath this glow.

He readies my bed and sweeps the matted floor,
sets forth hot soup and new-cooked rice.
This frugal meal deeply satisfies.

The night is still—all insects now are mute—
the clear moon climbs above the mountain top,
peeks through my shuttered door.

At dawn I wander, unsure of my path,
which twists and turns through mist and fallen snow.

Though tired and confused, I make a natural way,
with naked foot in azure streams
through alpenglow and stately giant pines
amid the gusts that roar
and flutter out my robe.

Content, I could grow old here,
shunning city ways. A student,
two or three, would find
an ancient soul
upon his proper path.

Sandra Ellston

蟬

To a Cicada
(after Li Shangyin)

You cannot sate your hunger
even on the tall grasses of summer,
and you are loath to chirp
in vain to empty ears.
By morning your song's grown weak—
the lone pine hears
but neither heeds nor cares.
I have drifted through life too long—
weeds choke my peaceful garden.
So vexed, I take to heart
your prudent reprimand—
to choose the genuine and simple way.

Ruth F. Harrison

Fireflies live dangerous

Fireflies live dangerous showy lives
are easy prey for bats and spiders.
A female *photurus* firefly mimics
the female *photinus*. When
the unsuspecting (oh, well: big,
dumb) testosterone-driven
male *photinus*
makes a pass
at the lady flashing in the grass
she eats him.

So far I have saved
the pines' yearly new candles,
red emperors, swallowtails,
wool carders, barbed wire,
owl and linnet and larkspurs,
moss flowers, a dragonfly
ant hills, my mother,
a brother and a cat

several rocks, a river,
and a canyon, but
the male *photinus* will
just have to look out
for himself.

Ruth F. Harrison

Hats

Hats will come back. One day
we will take seriously the thing
we know—most body heat is lost

through the head— and will call
them out of exile: *fedora,* we
will call, *homburg, Stetson* .... Our

shout will rise: *beret, fez, pillbox ...
shako, montera, panama ... turban,
beanie, cloche ... kerchief, cowl, cockade ....*

We will summon them: *bonnet, topi,* and *busby ...
helmet* and *tarboosh, ... leghorn* and *aigret ...
sombrero* and *hood* and *babushka,* we will

call them and they will come, with
a whooshing feltish leathery sound
of movement, will rise from their

historically brief nap in attic and trunk,
from hatboxes in basements, museums and
archives, rise crown and brim over woods

and meadows, across mountain and valley,
come seething up the city streets, from
attic and alley, will hover above us like

small copters, waiting, spying out
the land, and we will select ...
I say: dibs on the tricorn.

Ruth F. Harrison

In Fog White Blossoms Emerge Last

Scene: Being awake, I'm watching almost morning:
Wraiths of mist lift, swirl, descend, no wind
but air stirring and gray yet unabated;
shapes of evergreens loom flat as cutout--
black silhouettes on gray.

That woven wood fence assumes near-visibility
more by standing nearer than
some black shore pine, than of itself,
though a dim crisscross almost is.

Now deep-red begonias, no longer black on black
but color against wood-lath, celebrate
that eyes have cones, that cones awake with light.

Now, slow, the sweet peas rise from spiral fog, lift
yes pink blooms above the fence. ...Yellow now
non-stops loom up, leaning, spring
into fullness, mass and shape.

And Dawn in wet galoshes lights up heliotrope's purple,
impatiens' neon-pink.

Last of all arrive through trailed wisps
white stars of lobelia, against latticed and worn
wood. After such fine emergence, this freewheeling
dark yields mere and simple Thursday morning

a fact the grounded cloud contrived to soften
until fresh coffee signals common day.

Eleanor Berry

Found Objects

We choose such objects for some turn of grace
we'd like to own forever, close at hand
as lovers, though unwarm, unsentient, and
though statements they might make are made in place.
--Ruth F. Harrison, from "*objets d'art*"

We choose such objects for some turn of grace,
felicity of form that draws our glance
to linger, imagination to attach
itself, for something about them that by chance
resembles treasures lost we've longed to match.
We choose such objects for some turn of grace

we'd like to own forever, close at hand
as the cat curled each morning on our lap,
as music sounding deep within our chest
long after it's ceased. We choose what fills a gap
we'd scarcely felt, those few among the rest
we'd like to own forever, close at hand
as lovers, though unwarm, unsentient, and
inert. They keep us faithful company,
greet our arrival home, dispel our fear
of loneliness. In sunlight, lamplight, we see
their character come clear. They soon grow dear
as lovers, though unwarm, unsentient, and

though statements they might make are made in place
and without words, without expressive sound
or signifying gesture. They are the chorus
for the private drama of our days, profound

despite their quiet. They speak both to and for us
though statements they might make are made in place.

Eleanor Berry

In Defense of Analysis and in Praise of Horsechestnuts

If I watch the leaves come out
wet, green half-furled umbrellas
opening to make, each on its own,
a shelter, a shade,
seven leaflets radially splayed
to so broad a span;

if I tear
a sprig of three
small fringed flowers
from a tall
cream-white panicle, glowing
in the dusk of the big leaves,
and find one is yellow
at the center, one pink, one magenta;

if, sticking the sprig in water,
I discover next day the yellow
has pinkened, the pink
turned magenta, and surmise
all of the flowers must open

with yellow centers that change
daily toward a final purple;

if I focus
microscope at forty power
on a single anther, filling the field, see
its dust of pollen
is heaped
cinnamon-brown beads;

if, come fall, I split
one of the thorn-clad
pale green husks, put
the mahogany nut on my desk
and observe its shine
dulls in the air;

if, all winter, I study
the design of the stout
sparsely branched limbs—
curving down, then out
from the trunk, with a sharp
upturn at the tip—
giving the bare crown
a form as characteristic
of the species as the leaf's;

it is all to see the whole tree
clearly, clearly, as
multitudinously
one.

Eleanor Berry

Inland from the Edge

1

Ever since I followed
the Oregon Trail west
a decade ago, I've thought I lived
at the edge where the continent
ends in ocean.
But ninety miles inland
is not the edge.

The plants are different there
or grow differently
in sea-damp air.
Not tapering tops of firs
but thick, shelving limbs
of shore pines
rear against the sky,
lean permanently eastward
beneath the prevailing
wind off the sea.

In oceanside gardens,
misted by morning fog,
fuchsias reach the size
of rhododendrons inland,
roses and dahlias sport blossoms
wide as my hand spans,

leaves the circumference of saucers
set off superabundant
gold and orange nasturtiums—
as if the land
uttered itself fully
only in the face
of ocean.

2

A friend tells me how, years
before we met, when he was young
and bent on making art,
he emptied his savings
to rent a cottage on the coast
for three months. There,
working twelve hours
and eating one meal
a day, he completed almost a hundred
big still lifes, colored pencil
and cut paper, a single
huge series, mostly of flowers—

as if his carefully balanced
compositions of blooms in vases
in front of a half-closed blind,
his intricate cut-outs
of sheets of paper, spaced by heavy
sheets of glass, could hold back
the ocean. But the waves
broke in his head as they break
in a rock cave
at the edge of the land.

3

We could all
have been swept away
young, but that artist friend
now grows an inland garden,
and messages reach me
from my high school circle of rivals,
AP classmates I lost touch with
four decades ago.

From time to time, over
those years, I'd see their names—
in roundups of recent
advances in particle theory,
on the faculty roster for a top
medical school, in the music
production credits for films
that won at Sundance. Now I learn
the physicist has a daughter and son,
both in college; the research physician
worries for her mother, ninety-five,
a month in Intensive Care; the musician
has had AIDS for years, lost a lover,
dozens of friends, has more than once
been close to death himself.

Now the one whose vita
I never found on the Web
sends Williams' "This Is Just to Say"
as apology for not requiting
my story of my life
these past forty years
with a like tale of his own.

We could all have been
swept away young. I ask
about the one whose name
none of the others has spoken—
our group's irrepressible
brilliant mathematician. The answer
comes slow: *He
killed himself in college.*

4

The rest of those old classmates
get together at least
a few times a year.
They all live now
around where we grew up.
Since then I've put that place
three thousand miles
behind me. Strange to think
they stayed there, or went back,
inland from the opposite edge
of the continent between us.

Judith H. Montgomery

Saint Colonoscopy

Where there is no bright blood to follow,
I am blessed. Or not: not found out, not

snipped by the black snake that slithers

in, peering for apocalyptic growth
within the slick recesses of my flesh.

Not to be bleeding, not to be bled:

blessing conferred by my surgeon, her
kind eyes icy as God's while she searches

out fault in the garden. May no fruit bud

within this winding vine. May the snake
angel ever seek in vain.

Penelope Scambly Schott

He Nicknames What He Loves and Takes It Out to Dance

Ass candle
Battering ram
Crotch cobra
Divining rod
Eel
Fool sticker
Giggle stick
Hair splitter
Irish root
Joy stick
Kosher pickle
Lizard
Mister Bluevein
Nine-inch knocker
One-eyed pants mouse
Pump handle
Quim wedge
Rumpleforeskin
Sweet thumb of love
Tummy banana
Uncle Johnson
Vanquisher
Whore pipe
Xylophone hammer
Yum-yum
Zucchini

Now I've said my *ABC*'s,
tell me what you think of me.

Penelope Scambly Schott

In this high desert place of ill repute

a black locust tree
spills fragrant tiers
of white blossoms:
a bridal bouquet

a sweet girl like you
a smart girl like you
a pretty girl like you
 a girl like you
You in a place like this?

Dear sanctimonious Sir,
have you seen my long thorns?
Where is your flesh most tender?
Where is your skin most thin?

Penelope Scambly Schott

My Lover is the Ceiling

The ceiling is my lover
I gaze into its cracked plaster
I am transfixed
by yellowed ivory paint

I look unto heaven
whence cometh my salvation
Sometimes I don't remember
which man sweats on top of me

When I was a child
in a pressed white pinafore
I lay on the cool lawn
watching clouds float

If I thought a prayer
the clouds flipped below me
so I was lying upside down
high over heaven

Julius Jortner

Strategy

In a crowd
unlikely to be singled out
yet vulnerable to
mass movements or epidemic
we are not safe.

Standing alone
exposed on all sides
not safe either.

As I cling to you
have I shared the danger
or have I doubled my exposure?

At least we warm each other.

First place

Tim Whitsel
Mudflat Allure

Birds in the moist darkness.
A quintet of gulls sharks
for finger-length salt worms,
evening snacks as the tide
pulls away. Our lanterns
sizzle, flaring the abruption
of a blue heron making his
great-jointed ascent.

Working, at winter break.

Wool union suits scratch
young skin at the margins.
Our burlap bags will not freeze
while we kneel beside
dikes to rake for manila clams.
In deeper water, light
gleams, a small tugboat nags
at the vast corduroy of a log boom.

Fog hangs in rivers of night air.

Second place

Bill Siverly
November Home

Fog hangs in the branches, veiling yellow maple leaves.
Above the damp ground, wood smoke adds its caustic
bite to fog.
Grown daughters with their miseries of loneliness in
marriage
pause briefly in the driveway and then fly off on their
long migration.

Alone at last, we spend the afternoon nesting in bed.
We find refuge in old marriage, coming home from
previous lives.
Our hands of their own accord follow the intuition of
skin,
As if our bodies had known each other long before we
met.

Early darkness surrounds us like the breath of large
animals.
Eyes and thought shut down, we fly with unconscious
abandon.
Your Archaic smile just after sex is always the same.
Ancient wisdom shines in your eyes and hair like a
winter moon
as the pair of us glide to earth on synchronous wings.

Rain returns like a revenant visitor peering in windows.
"It rains gently on the town," Rimbaud said in a
previous life.

Time transforms everything, but in our hands
time comes to a standstill like the chime of a clock at
one.

Mist hovers in the evergreens, then drifts away on
autumn winds.
Against the damp chill we light a fire under a fir log.
We read and talk and savor autumnal peace, karma
complete.
We have found what it means to live on earth.

Third place

Joan Dobbie
Other Woman Monologue

I'm cast to be the Queen
of Darkness, bride of evil,
the wicked, other woman
in the play.

Not her, sweet charming beauty
in the center of the story
but the other, shadow woman.

The one who waits alone
in her lonely echoing house.
The one he comes to, now and then,
in the night, in secret,

whispering, "It's only me.
Don't be afraid." And then,
"She mustn't know.
For God's sake, please!
It would destroy me."

"And what of Hell?" you say.
I've been there.
And it wasn't wickedness
that got me in, but fear.

"And what of friendship
between women?"
Isis, hear me out –

I'm going blind.
"And what of love?"

I speak of hunger
& of music.
The song my body sings
when his nipples brush my breast.

His lips, his breath...
The ancient warbler's holy trill.
I think that I would die for this.
I know that I would kill.